Soultending

by
Meredith Briggs Skeath

Meredith Briggs Skeath, known as "Mer" to her family, was born in 1949, attended Harvard University and Indiana University as an undergraduate, received an M.A. from Maharishi University of Management and an M.F.A. in creative writing from Warren Wilson College. She has taught writing at the elementary, secondary, and college levels and has read her work in many settings, including the Library of Congress, Yale University, and on National Public Radio. Since 1971 she has also taught the Transcendental Meditation program. She lives in Silver Spring, Maryland with her husband and three children.

Copyright 2003 by Meredith Briggs Skeath
All rights reserved, including the right of reproduction in whole or in part in any form.

Printed by Glanzer Press, Newberry, Florida, USA

Cover photo: *Tulip Poplar Seed Cup* by Janet B. Briggs

Back photo: Perry R. Skeath

Acknowledgments

The author gratefully acknowledges these periodicals in which the following poems first appeared:

Contemporary Review: Grand Jeté
Radcliffe Quarterly: Giving Away the Layette
Triquarterly: The Two Doors at Either End of the Hall
Virginia Quarterly Review: Bridget McGonagle Briggs
Warren Wilson Review: Closing Ranks, Hunting Abstractions, To the Taj and Back, Watching the Cell Divide, The Wire Is Never Completely Taut
Ribbon of Song: WPFW's Poetry Anthology: Labor and Delivery: No Record

For my teachers—
foremost the Lord—and for all the Lord's proxies,
knowing and unknowing.

I was not aware of the moment when I first crossed the threshold of this life.

What was the power that made me open out into this vast mystery like a bud in the forest at midnight?

When in the morning I looked upon the light I felt in a moment that I was no stranger in this world, that the inscrutable without name and form had taken me in its arms in the form of my own mother.

Even so, in death the same unknown will appear as ever known to me. And because I love this life, I know I shall love death as well.

The child cries out when from the right breast the mother takes it away, in the very next moment to find in the left one its consolation.

Rabindrinath Tagore, *Gitanjali*, Section XCV

Contents

I. Loss

Permission 2

The Wire Is Never Completely Taut 3

Closing Ranks 4

Divining Caleb 7

The Two Doors at Either End of the Hall 8

Watching the Cell Divide 10

Grand Jeté 12

March 4th 14

Bridget McGonagle Briggs (1887-1913) 16

Poco a Poco 17

R.S.V.P. 19

April in Majorca: for Robin Parker 21

To the Taj and Back 22

Giving Away the Layette 24

No One to Bury 26

When I Die, Find the Children 27

After Words 28

II. Mothering
1. Child: Hard to Love As a Mirror

bodyfriend	30
i grow	31
I am no one's guardian	33
Warning: I am not	34
We will confront each other many times before we meet	35
oh ketchup faucet	36
Spring Mill State Park	38

2. Wife: The Cupped Hand

The Glade	40
Before the Concert	41
On the Continental Divide	42
Distinguishing You	43
A Cupped Hand	46

3. Mother: The Tree of Life

Strange As a Moon Rock	48
Projection	49
Fetal Stress Test	50
As Far As I Know	51
Pedigree	52
Labor and Delivery: No Record	53
Newborn Illusions	54

Maternal Development 57

The Hammer's Claw 64

You May Not Remember 65

Immersion 66

What I Learned Being a Mediocre Bookkeeper 68

God's Net 69

In Hiding 70

III. Courted by God
And underneath <u>are</u> the everlasting arms.
– Deuteronomy 33:27

Unexpected Call 72

Before and After Eating 73

Outside the Orchard 74

Hunting Abstractions 76

Sleeping Under Dogs 78

Attempted Translation 79

Wastebasket 81

What My Coach Said Before the Reading 82

Vitae 83

August Morning 84

Owning Up 85

I. Loss

Meredith Briggs Skeath

Permission

>from the Latin, "to send through"

I'll have to grant you passage through, with the smudge
of northern lights over your farm, the scruffy perennials—
foxglove, deer-lopped phlox—standing by.
Friends say you will need permission

to die. I wanted you to fight for your life
as if it were mine. "I'm not afraid of dying," you said, "just the mess
of dragging the family down."

Does the unknown you've never reduced
to God now play a largo in your ear,
make you willing to leave children who don't want you
to initiate them into death?

You want to expand the border
between treatments. I spade up clumped narcissus—
offspring, parent bulbs ajumble. You kneel,
pry them apart without shearing roots, heel them
embedded in bone meal, under separate,

new earth. Are you set on seeing them break ground
in April, spear and hoist dead leaves aloft,
or are you showing me, Mother, as I grip you
firmly under one arm to help you up,
that my longing holds you back?

The Wire Is Never Completely Taut

"This pole will be your best friend," my mother said,
balancing twelve feet of light aspen
in my hands. I step onto the high wire, its wavering line
earth spun into a black, narrow street.

"When you're alone eighty feet up, dirty sparrows dart,
kids below teeter on bleachers, are stopped
or fall, but the pole will keep you from thinking
of falling faces or almost anyone
you love. The aspen widens
your body, makes the narrow moment broad.
Only the groove the wire makes
through the rosined slipper will touch you."

                                                   She was right.
Time extends from the pole's ends,
slips out of mind into flapping duckcloth, diffused
uncertain light. I hear two favorite elephants—Sasha and Tibor—
trumpeting below on cue, rearing on two legs,
then one. I feel Mother hovering near their ring,
in remission, or balancing as I am, looking straight ahead.
Mid-wire, we curl our toes. I nod to the hands:
       take away the net.

Meredith Briggs Skeath

Closing ranks

Your umbilical cord corkscrewed
your life into mine: now what wrong turn
makes you recoil, misshape genes,
bulge as if I were still in you?

Driving home from the hospital white scarves
of snow wrestle in my headlights.
You pressed washrags to my forehead,
held me spindly over the sink
when I retched as a child.

"I'm no good as a nurse," you confessed,
slumping beside me in bed, queasy
from empathy. Now it's my turn to serve,
jam pillows behind your hips.
Why shouldn't you inhabit

the bell curve's far right end
reserved for survivors?
Even in sleep I look this tumor
in the eye—the black-eyed center
where it begins to die—
and wake with a clenched fist.

*

Your dog sniffs for your scent, not mine
each night when I come home from the hospital.
He retrieves you from the bouquet of antiseptic
and stomach fluids, then follows,
wagging, into the dark house.

I leave the screen door ajar
each morning so he can pace in and out,
sleep on your bed or the porch chaise
in wait for you, knowing you are somewhere
as autumn burns across the Berkshires.

※

The unused wig rests on its plastic head,
nightgowns lope over wicker.
Standing in the jamb I see myself writing the obituary,
then see you lifting my unborn children,
teaching them to open the Steinway's huge mouth,
press the first, tentative notes
from the long strings, the ivory world.

One instant your ashes are being sown in the meadow,
then you're back taking photos, one-woman shows mounting
across New England. A neon rainbow,
"terminal," strobes in my forehead. I dismantle it,
take down the milder, blue arch, "remission,"
shunt them both into my aorta
bulging from one pulse, then the next,
and walk into your undraped room to open a window.

※

If you have not died yet

I will bring my child to you when she is born.
The trees will be naked then.
We'll all be naked.

I go down on my knees among these houseplants
to pray that your life be spared.
The palm does not nod,
the cyclamen's flowers continue to open

toward the floor. I look down, up, in.
My heart, a bald stone,
cries in a desert.

Meredith Briggs Skeath

※

On either side of the zipper scar
your belly throbs. Will it flatten
with your female parts, all that tumor

gone? I bring you home from this cutting
away death. Who's whistling slow movements
from our favorite quartets? Death whispers,
"I am peaceful."

Knowing today I've rescued you
and you are still in my embrace
I can say, "Be gone."

※

Mother sent me on a walk alone,
my second since my daughter was born.
Strange not to carry her, arch my back
to balance her twenty-four pounds leaning out,

a strong-willed, tilting sailor.
Runners pumped past with Walkmen,
women behind strollers pushed their heart rates up,
seemed already out of the woods

or never to have entered them,
until I saw one woman carrying her newborn,
cradling its weak stem, the neck,
embracing the torso as tightly as possible

without pressing those soft bones.
Warming, calming the child, she could not bear
to do otherwise, the birth ringing her,
that descent still throbbing.

I passed unnoticed, summer air insulating
her feelings, light slanting down
between pillared tulip trees
a hundred and fifty feet to the green floor.

Divining Caleb

Months before we conceived you I sensed
your presence. After I became pregnant you approached
gradually, moving inside like a modest occupant
into a one-bedroom rambler with just enough furniture.
A doctor called: my mother was dying. In utero
you comforted me. Peace, as well as grief
can be bestowed. I don't know how, but it is

by you. I thought my mother's name, "Janie, Janie" pushing
you out. You came so fast, a hand to your cheek
as if reflecting even in that upheaval, birth,
the midwife had to hold you back. My mother stayed alive
to see you. Always precise
she exclaimed softly, "How perfect!"
cradling you on her dying belly. Was it your volley

of smiles that released her? She stopped breathing
after you fell asleep. No fear, no pain, a simple exit.
I stroked her hair, whispered like a loving fool
in her dead ear. My cousin telegraphed from England,
"All the trumpets sounded for her

on the other side." Caleb, prince Caleb
we named you after she died. Comforter, spy for God.

Meredith Briggs Skeath

The Two Doors at Either End of the Hall

FOR MY FATHER

The two doors at either end of the hall
        are usually locked.
In the midst of feasting
        I notice with fascination
not the lush red velvet arms of the chairs
        or the small green curls
on top of the toothpicks piercing the cubes
        of muenster and strawberries.
I don't smell the brazier broiling
        the red flesh brown, or hear
the question, "How do you like living
        in Washington?"
I don't feel the outside
        of my heel wearing down
        so I tilt, not quite vertical
through the hall.

I am looking out the second door, opened a crack
        since you died,
looking at the unlit depth, sure
        the air beyond is the air
I'm breathing, the space the same
        as the space within the lush appointments
        of the feasting hall—
        only unencumbered.

The waiter in tails asks me if I care for a slice
        of prime rib. Amid the clinking,
lobbyists are jockeying toward the host,
        trailing a wake of cologne and hair spray
like an aura
        you slipped out of. No one here has noticed you
are commanding my attention:
        I look toward the dark,
firm line showing through the door.
        I walk toward it

not afraid but wanting
> a guide to that language
that souls may speak when mouths are gone,
that whales may hear, perhaps a higher frequency,
or a different law, that birds may know
flying above the buildings and under the planes,
or plants may sink their roots into,
the dark shiftings, the ooze
of underground springs. Where have you gone?
> What gifts can I bring you?
> What sign can you share?
I love the light I have known here, but will come
> wherever you are, if I could speak with you
and know the builder
> of the hall.

Watching the Cell Divide

ROBERT WILLIAM BRIGGS (1911-1983)

I.

You studied embryos, bent
over a microscope examining dishes
of frogs' eggs 'til ten
most nights, sometimes plucked
their nuclei out with a micropipette
to edge your way into life's beginnings,
how one cell became many,
what went wrong
when a cancer grew.
DNA was more real to you
than the calendar, the checkbook, or whatever
the church handed down about God.

II.

Before I could walk you put me on top
of the piano and played me to sleep.
High on the black plateau, the scratchy
Mexican blanket under my legs,
I felt the music—Haydn—
pitch through my spine and hips. I wanted
to get down, felt only
helpless and the strain
of your music through me, only a fear
that I was more to you
than a child should be.

III.

Thirty years later you watched
your second wife walk to a bus,
pause at a neighbor's willow
to see how the one she'd just planted
would look in a year or two.
You felt me watching
and turned. "She has a spirited,
definite walk," you said smiling,
as if to explain, and sat down, opening
the paper on your knees.
I read your face: seventy, finally
fully in love.

IV.

On our last motorcycle ride into the Indiana hills,
slanting into the curves
you suddenly stopped,
pulled off your helmet. Through the whoosh
of wind you had heard
spring peepers chorus.
With ears twice as old as mine
and cancer growing in your groin, you had heard,
and I had noticed nothing.
Driving back, helmeted in dusk,
no one else on the road, you drove
into a swarm of fireflies. You slowed,
hoping not to hurt them.
In a cloud of light, by thousands
they took us in and crowned you
as I couldn't, though I wanted to.

Grand Jeté

You had sent me a picture of Makarova leaping forward,
the ground out of view, her legs split
in midair, the caption, "A dancer hates
the floor," but you can only lie down
or sit as you die. Speech dismantled,
sunlight takes on a different hue, as in an eclipse.
We don't remember our birth, that door,
unless we are gifted, but an electric walkway
is carrying us toward the other one.
We do not notice. Surely it is the trees, the days
outside that are moving, not us.
Then someone opens the door through which only he
can see, as if death were an eyelid opening.

I wanted as a child to go behind the waterfall at Bash Bish,
stand in the hidden recess,
in back of perpetually falling water and sound,
in a cave of quiet.
Perhaps you have gone behind such a curtain.

We still set at times one too many places
at the table and cannot listen
to the records you loved.
You left no access
except an ambiance I've felt before
when you asked me twice
if I were happy, because you were slightly drunk
and wanted to be sure.
Your nature roared up
in my cells when you died, not to finish a life
for you, but to *be* you
in the world, in disguise.

Since then I've read of those revived from clinical death.
I know that time drops away, an artifact.
Motion slows, and peace, as when I lay
in New Delhi, my brain at 105° and climbing—
a visceral, cellular peace reasserts itself,
a backdrop moving forward.

But how can I assume it is the same
for you? I picture you waltzing
with your wife, but no one has returned
to say you found her when she died this April.
Before you died I saw you open your eyes wider,
take a good look through the morphine gauze,
as if you were taking, not just us,
or your own life, but the whole world along.

March 4th

Holding the hand of the dead man,
my father, I closed my eyes and meditated.
We still might share internal silence.
The social worker came for my stepmother, the doctor came
to feel the wrist, the head nurse rolled down the bed
before my father stiffened sitting up.
But death had not occurred in a moment

and was still going on, the eyes still open,
the body shutting down province by province, the blood slowing
before it stopped. I held his hand for that final
settling of cells, long after breath ceased
and EEG went blank. The nurse brought a pitcher
of orange juice and left. My brothers talked
in low tones; we had not been together
alone in one room for years. My stepmother went to call
whoever needed to be called, not wanting to see
his body swollen and staring, that used to be slim,
bounding up stairs two at a time.
And his booming laugh, that's what she wanted in her mind,
not this silence. When I opened my eyes
the hand in mine was cooler, no longer my father's.

The nurse gave us a box of kleenex, suggested we go
have breakfast at Howard Johnson's; she would stay with him.
It was early morning, the first day in March
that felt like spring, with a high, vaulting blue sky.
"It feels like Florida!" said the woman in the next booth.
We ordered; Evan got an eyelash in his scrambled eggs
and ate methodically around it. We laughed, giddy,
suddenly hungry. No one seemed to notice
that I had *become* my father—my eyes and their rims red,
my ankles swollen, arms lead. Surely they saw

Soultending

my gestures now were his, that he had commissioned me,
and the half of him in me was already leaning out
after him, as the sea does with the moon. I had to call it back,
pick it up, dead in each cell, and breathe into it,
hoping, if I kept the relic alive, it would rise
to the surface someday, and keep rising
and take the rest of me with it.

Bridget McGonagle Briggs (1887-1913)

I don't look like my mother or father,
but like a grandmother who died fifty years before I was born:
genes like dolphins surface unpredictably.
Her unschooled ballerina's posture, her hair swept up leaves
her forehead clear. She's looking slightly
to one side of the lens, not breathing,
holding her eyelids and mouth still
without strain, as if this were an ability
she often used, but no one ever remarked upon.

Her cheek bones curve elegantly
toward her poised mouth.
At the neck of the laced, white,
high-collared blouse, a single brooch.
Maybe she brought it from Ireland two years before
and is looking, without regret, in that direction,
remembering Donegal, or imagining her upcoming marriage,
her next emigration, from her own mother
and sisters, to join the man who wanted this picture.

Surely she is not looking ahead to me,
or to her two sons, or to the one who will survive
when she and the other son die of TB.
Her face, though tempered, is not expecting
trouble. She can settle
a colicky child, an uneasy horse,
but after this sitting she moved on
soon to go under, curving toward me.

Poco a Poco*

FOR BLANCHE BLOCH (1890-1980)

When my grandmother became round
shouldered as a gourd, her withered belly
pushed forward by her collapsing spine,
I kneaded her shoulders,
brushed her hair—long,
white, thick to the end.
When she slumped, desolate,
a lake of saliva and vacant age,
I rushed, knelt, took her head
in my hands, brought her back to the room,
before dinner, with the Bach she had played
on the radio, and her great grandson
clattering in the kitchen.

She insisted I wake her
before I left for the five a.m. plane.
Deep beyond dreams, her mouth was gaping.
"Nana," I whispered.
She lurched up, open-eyed,
and bugled "God bless you!"

Since then I've spoken to that part of her
when she couldn't remember
how to put in her teeth,
or poured water down the toaster,
or asked "How old am I? What does it matter?"
on her birthdays. I honed in on her
underneath senility, the broken hip,
the osteoporosis we mistook as inevitable.

*a musical term, from the Italian, meaning "little by little"

Meredith Briggs Skeath

My mother said Nana was reaching up and out
as if climbing rope, moments
before she died. A thousand miles away
I felt her—toothless,
scot-free, flinging boons.
Half with her beyond her death,
I saw fear collapse, as her spine had
to small lumps of bone no thicker
than crinoid stems. I wrapped myself
in her Viennese shawl
rampant with flowers
and walked outside, no longer needing
any destination.

R.S.V.P.

FOR CHRISTOPHER BLOCH

Today is the day you'll wake up, remember
not the steering wheel granite heavy
on your chest, but the airy quilt
of altocumulus clouds, the way deer approach
your cabin at night, and the peal
of your wife's laugh coming out the bright window.
Today is the day you'll come
back into your body, pick up the pieces,
help the mechanic knit your bones, pump your lungs.

When you can breathe on your own
they're going to play God with your face,
so we took them a picture of how you used to look
told them you wouldn't want to come out
like a Marlboro man, a good
Bloch nose and cheek bones were hard to come by.
After surgery they say you'll be able to talk.

Your sister's flying in from London
with the son she named for you.
The children are being taken care of,
we held hands in a circle and want to see your hands
around a coffee mug again.
Everyone's asleep now, breathing as uneventfully
as you will breathe soon, easy in,
easy out, but I'm awake, wanting
to pull you through,
your red, thick bush of hair
matted on your unconscious head.

There is only the slightest shift
in genes from you, cousin, to me: years of using
the same forks at our grandparents,
hide-and-seek around the same spickle bush,

Meredith Briggs Skeath

defending each other for doing work we loved
which didn't pay. The lower meadow was strewn with bodies
of old Corvairs you dissected to build your inventions.
Deep in debt, you drove me a thousand miles
to see my father and wouldn't let me pay
for even a meal. You stood by the stove,
tamped tobacco in your pipe,
spoke of wanting to bring your new wife
to your cabin up the mountain,
with its view of the Berkshires, its frozen pipes,
and no insulation, one room you were sure you could build on.
You called the doctor when I collapsed
on a Manhattan street. Whom can I call for you,
now that all the doctors have come, hovered, and left?

April in Majorca: for Robin Parker

Alone with my life
the moonlight combed her dark hair
and it became mine.
—Robin Parker (1950-1971)

I went to the sea cliffs
when I heard you had killed yourself:
an April storm took what it would.
This island has grown smaller,
lost its edge to the sea.
Now brittle bushes quiver, push
their waxed, yellow flowers into twilight.
The workmen have gone from the cove.
Clouds come, cover the stars, wash away again,
reveal what was always there.
I nudge the earth; pebbles
avalanche over the side.

I saw you the first time you jumped and lay
flat on an Oakland street,
mumbling "I promise"
to someone I could not see.
You said talking to me
was like talking to the earth,
but neither earth nor I could ease you.

Now swallows fly below me, in tiers above the water,
catching insects in a flying, dark net.
Neatly death comes, so far below,
in the midst of grace.
The moon pushes up from the sea,
a tongue of light.
I wonder whether you looked down
or up as you fell.
I hope you felt eternity in the fall,
no pain, just a settling in.

Meredith Briggs Skeath

To the Taj and Back

FOR ANDREW JOSEPH WEISER (1949-1988)

We traveled to India, our joy unalloyed
as the unfast dyes swirling the hems
of saris in the narrow, cow-crowded streets
that reeked of God, devotion, feces, wood smoke and diesel.
Holding hands, we ran across hysterical traffic
as innocent, bonded friends with maps of each other
like planetarium constellations glowing
on our inner walls. Cholera, dysentery—somehow
we were exempt. We went to the Taj
because you had dreamt of its lines
in architecture school as one might dream
of a woman or the curve of a pear
after three months of fruitless winter.
Pollution dragged on the minarets,
discoloring the inlaid jewels' rose gleam,
but you saw it as it was intended, as you saw me.
Coming back we walked beside an elephant
lumbering amidst bleating taxis, to stay
in the air fanned by his tattered,
gigantic ear, to worship him in our wordless way.

When I woke, I forgot this dream, took my daughter
to the stream to wade barefoot for the first time
on a silt bottom, each step going deeper,
until silt swirled and I could not tell
what might lie ahead, glass or beer can tabs,
and I swept her up and took her back
under the bridge to hear runners,
dogs, and bikes clatter overhead.
Then I remembered I had not taken that trip with you,
but was forced to let you go,
how I held you for the last time,
each step you took going deeper, and away.

Soultending

As I tried to imagine you this evening, five days dead,
the gray sheeting in my brain gave way,
and for a moment an arched space appeared
where you seemed to be, almost laughing,
enfolded by light. Grief was displaced,
a joke. At the nub of feeling, where need
and praise are one, *before* the pull
of lesser loves, those lilliputian anchors staking me
to earth, I could see it might be the right time
for anyone to die. Then I was back
as quickly as a quarter turn of my wrist
closes the slats of the blind, parts the inner
from the outer world, where loss is real.

Meredith Briggs Skeath

Giving Away the Layette

FOR CAROL AND DAN

The aqua silk kimono
you sewed for Theresa you pass to me
and stumble, crying, upstairs.

We keep coats on but won't go
like thieves with the loaded bag
of baby clothes, the changing table,

the Christmas cookies wrapped
on top. Your husband turns to us
from wiping windows enclosing the fire

and says, "You can see the flames
clearly now." You come down
minutes later. When I praise your tree-angel

you start crying again and say,
"This isn't working."
After twelve miscarriages, you carried

Theresa to term.
She had a room with pink silk sheets,
embroidered, a tiny sweater of many colors

you knit. You clothed her with your body,
rocked her to sleep cradled
in your pelvis. Two years later

going into the attic for her things
engulfs you: stillborn.
You wave me away

saying, "You shouldn't be around
this kind of thing."
But I've spent my pregnancy nursing

Soultending

my mother through cancer as you plied me
with casseroles through four months
of nausea. My daughter will be born

with death growing in her bones
and will not be afraid.
As she sits in me, indissolubly connected,

we will sit by you, if it will help,
for however long it takes.
Your labor is not yet over.
Mine will be light.

Meredith Briggs Skeath

No One to Bury

No name to pass down.
Miss
carry: God threw me a pass,
I fumbled the ball,
and like every other fumbler
I'm left empty-handed, a failure,
burying you in my own blood
until your dead body, miraculous,
small as a cheap pencil sharpener,
disintegrates and seeps out.
Red

the color of grief—my eyes,
my blood, my clothes.
I took no credit for bearing three children into life:
    could I even shift
one cell, let alone make one? Likewise this failing
is not fully mine. I tried to welcome,
to help the miracle.

Your soul, unassuming, pure, never
entered the body. I called you little
flower and did my best to build
a body worthy of a saint. Tomorrow
I will bake you a cake and light
one candle, to grow on.
We'll use our best china, for even
my toddler, and I'll give my living children a lap harp to play
to buoy you with love as you recede

toward another woman
who can build a body to carry you
into a life you desire,
into a life you deserve.
Godspeed.
God bless you.

When I Die, Find the Children

or grandchildren, whoever are children then.
Offer to watch them. Wait until you're alone with them—
outside is best.
Ask them, "Bury me."
They will tumble on you, layered and raucous.
Give them that license
to be themselves.

Spend half the day, every day,
with them until life is printed on you
when you wake. One or another may kiss you then
and you will be drawn
back into your body
and give up wanting

to follow me.
Ask those who come to mourn,
instead to befriend a child,
in my name, for life.

Meredith Briggs Skeath

After Words

Grief, like our own life, has a life of its own.
It cannot be controlled.
If we let grief burn through us, though, both it and we will evolve.

All of us have been, or will be, as Isiah said, well "acquainted
 with grief."
From it surge our most pressing questions
 that can only be answered, not by the intellect,
 but by direct experience of what does not die.
For some grief becomes the spur to passionate spiritual growth.
 This is its hidden blessing.

If anything I've written brings you the comfort of knowing you are not
 traveling alone, or helps you open to your own immense
 feelings and their source, I will be very grateful.
May you be blessed.

Soultending

II. Mothering

1. Child: Hard to Love As a Mirror*

---

*Why poems about childhood, adolescence, and single adulthood under the rubric of mothering? We must learn, even as children, how to mother and nurture ourselves, and how to allow ourselves to be nurtured in turn by the Divine.

Meredith Briggs Skeath

bodyfriend

oh ribbed ark without
the sea, caught
in the invisible flood,
consider yourself
the dove, unknowing
but finding
your way.

i grow

tired
of growing
of sex the drying
glue which binds
in moist imagining
sleep I jerk awake
and know: I was desire
shriveling years ago.

i ruptured winter
not expectant spring.
wobble
i was born barely
past the frog
into gloves which put me
under glass, as sand into
the timer, to climb
but never out.

i sleep under my eyes
i wake when pushed
above the sea
to circulate as air
breathed in
postureless I run out
of doors
of air
of time

expired you say
slow down
another nervous habit
i won't keep
you past time
i've an alcoholic's soul

Meredith Briggs Skeath

wishing to be
anonymous
the mask in mirrors
past medicine
i swallow sound
to pound it into silence.

I am no one's guardian

no one's keeper. There're enough
animals in my own caves.
Too many for me to tame.
They roam loose, howling
into breasts, arching
into feet, lying down
into a stomach, dripping
into legs. I am alive
and populated, a mass
of feeling, a circuitry
of ill-worked energy;
the soul is hiding somewhere
here, waiting for a signal
that I am safe, that my outer
regions are ready
for the fragile
voice of who
I am.

Meredith Briggs Skeath

Warning: I am not

easily opened, digestible,
cold-pressed
ham;
not easily bent back
into shape,
no first offender;
not an easily mended
crotch;
not easily gained
or lost as your tan.
You lie
around me fingering blades
of grass, skittish
as a setter
afraid to come;
once come
afraid to stay.
But you are right to hesitate:
I have cold hands
and am as hard to love
as a mirror.

We will confront each other many times before we meet

in the subway staring down the line
at the frozen foods counter
    wondering whether orange juice is really necessary
at the dining room table
    turning away from another day without mail
in the bathroom
    catching a glimpse and wondering when complexions finally clear
at the midnight toning of Christmas mass
in bed
    thinking what glory minor prophets have known
    waiting for the *first* coming, not the second
of anyone I can unload my strength and weakness on
of anyone I can believe in
of anyone who can accept the giver without feeling delivered
of anyone who will take the second lead in the dialogue
    that has risen to my bedroom ceiling for three years
    the coming
of anyone who can siphon off a need to love
    without asking why the need is there
    without thinking such a need strange, or excessive, or anything
        but human
of anyone who can withstand a rebounding relief that should
    but may not presage a lasting loyalty
of anyone who can take me
    not ruthlessly, but knowingly
knowing my past is irrelevant, finished
knowing I am of scant substance
    having lost the habit of introspection
knowing that futures are for the insecure
    or those capable of planning their lives—
        I am neither.
Knowing all this, he will throw it aside
    for it says only what I am not
and he will come and lighten my laughter
and we will have no need of prophecy.

Meredith Briggs Skeath

oh ketchup faucet!

Blood is running out
of baby bag! Relief!
relief!
I'm no mother
this month

here it's out!
between my legs the end
of the fantastic joke:
I am
I'm not
I am
I'm not

toting a spittle
of cells already
printed,
wrinkled,
curled and ready
for eyes,
to float out of me
into blazen
lungcry air!

My blood leaves me
quietly as
a procession leaves
church. I wasn't ready
to bear you.
Is that why
there was no meeting
of souls inside me?
Why I am emptying
compact as a fist,
unwinding into my own life?

Soultending

Child who is not yet,
I am preparing a way
for you, making a bed
to cushion you
into life
strong-limbed
and shouting gladness
to be born!

When I am pure
you will come,
dipped from the root,
shooting into me,
shoot of my breast,
peace of my heart,
I will shuttle you
the best morsels,
the finest air;
I will serve you,
build your arms and
legs so you may
kick and leave me
completely!

Joyous, strong-
winded light,
I am the lamp polishing
myself to let you
through.

Meredith Briggs Skeath

Spring Mill State Park

After all
perception (love)
changes (the bud)
opens
        closes
(red)
        bellied.
        Nothing can
be predicted
precisely
                except
(love)
        as gravity
        (the ground)
                which we are
        planted in
                grow from
and toward.

2. Wife: The Cupped Hand

Meredith Briggs Skeath

The Glade

Midway up the mountain, ground almost marsh,
birches took over, white as neighbor's girls at the start
of summer, bending and straightening over ferns,
cinnamon, sensitive, interrupted.
Greens all had gold in them, the look of sun,
and moss wherever I lay.
A red fox was loping on a deer path,
testing the air; the wind blowing toward me
or the peace of the place
let him pass me by, unafraid.

I've often looked for that glade
to show my husband and lie down with him there,
to see if he felt the same
desire when we left to return to that spot.
But I've never found it again.
Maybe the succession of trees has altered it
beyond recognition. Maybe I no longer need
to hear what it told me I could be:
an enemy to no one.

Before the Concert

Sitting beside you, seeking assurance
I press my palm over your heart,
your swimmer's heart with its slow,

royal pace, never ruffled,
an andante fit
to accompany ladies in Haydn's court,
their stiff taffeta

pivoting gracefully around extended arms.
Each measured beat slows
the clock, conducts me
into calm. I lay my head

on your collarbone, the broken,
unset place that healed itself
with a small lump of bone,
the way you mend me

from the inside, without cast
or prescription, so I might believe
I alone with grace compose my life.
I cannot see your face,

but feel your smile spread,
as the orchestra tunes
to that one, clear note.

Meredith Briggs Skeath

On the Continental Divide

The divide isn't a mountain, just a matter of inches.

In our life below
I stopped paying you
complete attention the day I kept forking yams
my back to the door when you came in.
Autumn wasn't a season that year;
the first green leaf let go
before warring trees opened fire.

I started growing younger
when I looked up long enough
to see which way clouds were moving
and how fast. You came back
into focus, not in an embrace,
but when I took time to sit and simply watch
you shave, lean toward the mirror
concentrating on those hard hairs to get
at the end of your chin. Buzz
filled the room. I watched the fine cuttings
settle down like your feelings, a nearly invisible rain
I wanted to catch, protect, retain.

Above the Sierras we see a satellite blip
across the southeast quadrant. Shift
two seconds of arc and it would cinder
to earth or hurl off, going nowhere
in a straight line.

The thinnest stone I've found up here
will skip farthest across a pond.
I attend to the tip
of feeling, the way last light reflects
off your glance, off the mica rift,
the barely perceptible that divides
starting to die
from beginning to live.

Distinguishing You

FOR PERRY

I.

Sometimes in sleep we assume the same shape,
with knees bent like two skiers on the downhill
suddenly reposed above the drift.
You drape an arm around my waist
in the same slow, instinctive way my mother's German shepherd places his
large paw on her knee.
He leaves it there, knowing it means something to her—
just that it turns her toward him,
prompts her to stroke him from the top of his head
down to his shoulders. He waits through all this,
his paw still on her knee, wanting nothing but this,
not food, not a bed, not his world of scent outside,
only this.

II.

I have known a man who rolls away, a pillow in his arms,
when he's waking, finishing a dream of some other man
    he loves,
or a dream of music, the way it can fill him.
He lives apart from me and remote
from how he seems when he dresses and bends
over a blueprint, considering how the light
will enter the home he's just created.

And I've known a man who seems to rise laboriously
through layers of sleep as if he were passing
through each phylum—slowly,
slowly opening his eyes, bewildered
that sleep has washed him ashore on this world
    so tenuously connected
to what he has felt and longed for in the night
without being able to recall that country.

And I've known a man who instantly puts on formality,
    clears his throat
and stumbles to the bathroom, as if sleep is something
to be put out of mind, something that never existed,
    as if he is simply
a bit late for a meeting. He puts on his gestures,
then his concerns, the furrows
of what he has meticulously built for himself
painting the world not in dreams but in colors
    he can recall
from day to day, as a corner of a room might be recalled more easily than
its window.

I have always been shy to see people wake,
thinking their nature would show then,
    and it was as intimate
a glimpse as seeing them naked
or mumbling an apology after a quarrel. Waking up—
    who is taught
how to wake up, who can fake what shows then, before
    he remembers
his name, what was pressing, or even where he is?

III.

I remember you as if I had absorbed you through the skin,
and you persist, as my sense of myself does, in quietness
    through the night.
When you wake it is slowly, without rush.
You do not need to speak
but roll toward me, put your head on my shoulder,
    too bony
to be more than a temporary pillow, and I can watch you
gain alertness, as a heron might take flight,
its long legs waving with each wing beat,
    heading up into day.

You don't go to a hidden world, or an angry one,
    when you sleep.
I look at you as if I were seeing my own body

Soultending

and can't focus on you as if you were a separate being,
    and that is why
I take time to watch you sleep, or wake,
    or walk away
up the street, to see your gait, your spirit resting
    in itself,
and even then I see you carrying me as I carry you,
interfused as when we lie down, the same repeating curves,
    together.

A Cupped Hand

   the moon
hangs in the west, dipping gold
then deeper gold from the setting sun,
like the promise
of deepening love

   you have become.

   More flimsy now than ever,
our bodies fade as love courses in
and out of them, as picket fences
thrown up across the surging plains
fade, then fall, taken over.

   If my body's life were a child's

   summer vacation I'm starting August,
if my life is long. What use will I make
of the few long days of August?
What little change we'll see
when one body, then the other

   stops,

for we live now
in the core of our being.
(When we throw off a sheet
in the night we
still remain.)

   I will find you the same then

   only uncontained
and I will rise within and around you
to embrace you—without shaving,
deodorant, or food—the embrace will be the same as now,
in the cupped hand we've come to know.

3. Mother: The Tree of Life

Meredith Briggs Skeath

Strange As a Moon Rock

in me, fingerprinted sailor floating in dark,
I felt joy bolt from you like fire
from a Gatling gun, or chunks of light
shot through a fence.

I felt you turning
me toward you, as a sculptor turns
the cheek of a model to catch the light—
cream here, rose where the ear blooms.
I'd thought you were in my grasp.
Now who is shaping whom?

Projection

Eight months pregnant, afraid, I seem to hear
the child inside warning: "Get your life in order
I'm about to take over. You'll rob your own bones
to make milk for me, talk to me in tongues
like a Pentacostal, crawl on floors, rock me
'til your arms ache and still not sleep
because you'll be listening

"for me as for Elijah or a hidden god you know is coming
to demand your life, promising only
to outgrow you, live longer, be more powerful,
take everything and make you glad for it, make you feel
robbery as a gift. The muscles up your middle
are already being pulled apart,
weak lips over a secret.

"You won't know what I left to come here,
only what you've been stripped of—a prior, half-
life dangling on the earth, able to waste and plan
and take time as if you possessed it.
I'll root you deep, make you sniff out God
in the smell of my new skin, see Him in the sunburst
of stretch marks I've etched on your belly, feel Him
in your hips I've loosened like a lover
to make my passage. You will want to be,
more than anything, the wings of an angel over my life."

Meredith Briggs Skeath

Fetal Stress Test

My uterus contracts. Your heart rate jumps: 140,
160 beats a minute. "Responsive, looks good.
I want to see how ripe you are," the midwife says,
sticking a gloved hand up my vagina,
tapping your head through the closed cervix.
You jerk away. "Not engaged yet.
Do whatever you can to deliver this weekend."

Home now, my roofing skin stretches
to admit the sun. Deep as gold
in the South African imagination, you jut out
a limb. I press my skin above it.
You push out buttocks. I massage you,
stop. You punch out, wanting more.
I massage ten minutes while you rutch,
then sink into sleep. Jellied
like a museum calf, come,
bring that turquoise cord down with you.

As Far As I Know

FOR JOANNA ARIEL

You were born not loving
the world; it fell to me to court you
with folds of warm skin, mounds of breast
to finger, squeeze as you sucked

the steady stream. Even before you were born
I connived to catch you,
create from free-spinning DNA the drive
to live. At eight months I strode over dunes

to reach the Atlantic, splashed up to my knees,
pointed my belly straight into the spume
of winter tide sucking me
out to sea and said,

"The OCEAN, little one, the OCEAN,"
as if its surge would lure you
to love the world as I was confident,
even then, I could make you love me.

Meredith Briggs Skeath

Pedigree

God opened me, taking more than a rib
to make you and the radiant heat
from your soft-shelled brain.
With hands just fashioned in the dark,
wet workshop, you come staring.

From where?
The down spiral nebula
on the crown of your head gives one clue,
your toes' prehensile grasp another.
Suckling, incipient saint,
which are you? Which am I?

Labor and Delivery: No Record

If the birth was easy or hard,
no one knows. She was great
with child, and without.
The infant, like most, was flushed,
his entrance shooting
unmapped, underwater rapids.

Suck, my child,
and the afterbirth pulsed out.
Wasn't she foremost a mother,
cord and blood soaking
into her gown? Her voice curved around the child
not carrying
even as far as her husband, that good man
who had no part in this.

The child's skull was as soft
as any mortal's. Did he navigate
around the sternum, through that compressing
vise vagina into the open
without a dent? Did he nurse,
sleep well? Only animals
could be unintrusive enough
to help him gather himself
for his life's unreeling. A woman trundled out
from the inn to clean up.

Meredith Briggs Skeath

Newborn Illusions

    1. The bedridden newborn is inert, like other invalids.

My daughter thrashes all limbs in concert,
like an aquadancer at the Y. She churns her new element,
air, into a sweat of urine and tears,
bent on commanding those neurons racing
toward her feet.

    2. Nursing recreates the Madonna's aura—
      mother tenderly holding, child tenderly sucking,
    the pale liquid passing between them, an unseen transfusion.

This child latches on with fury,
her grip tighter than a surgeon's clamp:
hunger is the one sensation,
the world to be conquered.
My gnashed nipple arches, stiffens, bleeds.
I pant as if in labor, my feet
thrash against the floor
from pain, like dying fish.

    3. The infant sleeps peacefully.

This infant flails her arms and snorts,
capable of rousing all adults within earshot, catapulting us
to cribside. "Is she breathing?
Are her feet warm enough?
Has she wet?"
A smile passes before she sinks into dreams, the way station
between her source and this landing,
this strange new net of eyes and hands.
Fist swallowing, lip smacking,
rapid jaw movements, this is sleep.
Does she tremble, like the rest of us,

from her history? She may be innocent,
but she was never blank.

    4. There is one kind of sucking.

First she gulps milk, wheezing it in,
than sucks deeply while her eyes roll up.
Next small sucks like tucks in a hemline,
afterthoughts with long pauses to admire the material,
to rest from the work of sucking her meal out of another animal.

In dreams she twitches as she sucks,
mouthing the words from a hidden script.
Chewing, kissing and more will come,
but all from this single contact
when food came in a steady stream,
gushing when we pressed for it, naked and warm.

    5. The newborn does not smile.

When I simply stroke her beginnings of hair
she smiles without blinking into my eyes,
as if God were in her telling me, "Yes,
you are loved for being, not doing,
just as you are in your milk-stained gown,
crumpled, bleary with matter in your eyes,
angry from brute fatigue when you can carry,
hold, caress no more, when no rocker
rocks long enough for her." How can anyone
smile like that at me?

    6. Never take your infant to bed with you.

Remember the night I almost fell out of my prescribed rocker,
nearly crushing you as I nursed properly, sitting up?
Now you sleep between me and my husband, our brain waves
synchronized—I wake a few seconds before you.
I dissipate a bad dream in ten seconds,

take away hunger by rolling toward you and unbuttoning.
We sashay through the night, the three of us rolling
into each other's arms and away
to sculpt our own sleep and dreams.
You wake smiling, thrilled, four arms
to welcome you back.

7. Newborns don't see well.

I've caught you looking out
of this world—an astute stare.
Am I to judge what you see
by my gated eyes, by the visible spectrum,
that slip smaller than a nickel's filling?
You came fresh-minted and bear the stamp
of origins. How did Eden smell?
Like your skin.

8. The newborn has no esthetic preferences.

You prefer Matisse to Vermeer, Fra Angelico
to baby books, a cappella to orchestras,
slow movements to prestos. You want to be held facing out
to look intently at a table cloth, a parent,
an orange juice squeezer. You listen
to prayers attentively, to scripture, to any tone of voice
that spells peace and prefer, above all others,
the picture of your father holding you.

Your tastes are as specific as a gardenia's,
but you may remember none of this.
Like a prophet of origins with a steaming urn to conjure up a past
you are beholden to, but cannot name,
I will tell you how you emerged, unhesitating,
making a decision at every turn.

Maternal Development

    One Month: Milk Addict

In an earthquake you'd be found latched on
to your nipple of choice, drinking milk
as ash settled, inhaling sweetness as air darkened.

It took you two days to realize nipples
were not detachable and a face, mine in this case,
went with them. Last night I slunk to bed
like a member of an endangered species,
cowering to elude you, but every three hours you opened an eye,
spotted me. Wobbling your large head,
you wrenched my body, lying in state
to an upright position where, with only primeval
brain activity, I supported your neck
as I lifted you, your fists
clenched white with hunger.

Before you drifted off you stopped nursing
to look, long and intently, at my wedding ring.
Did the night light off the gold please you?
What shapes did your thought take, quicker than words?
As you fell asleep you raised your hands in mudras
the East has tried for three thousand years
to codify. Who were you saluting at that small gate
to heaven you frequent?

    Four Months: You've divided creation into unsuckable,

suckable, and eminently suckable items. You're still working on detaching
your ears and stuffing them in your mouth.
If I speak while you nurse you pull off solemnly:
"Surely this lapse could not have been
premeditated, Mama." I stop talking. The phone rings.
I don't answer it. I eat quiet foods: pablum,

cottage cheese. Your father opens his corn chip bag
in the basement. Celery has been banished forever.
When sated you lurch off the nipple with a smacking kiss,
flinging one arm back. Roses should be flung
at your operatic, pea-sized toes,
squirming while you tank up. Come,
stuff my body in your mouth.
Let me feel you forever.

    Six Months: A glacier coursing across the living room,

you sweep everything into your mouth.
I lapse into a recurrent hallucination: you're Brahman
the all-devourer, compacted into a seventeen-pound
masquerade: baby girl with two incisors.
When I found a fuzz ball from our new carpet
and a bit of the yellow pages in your b.m.
I thought, "She needs closer surveillance."
When the diaper looked eerily like a Roerschach test
as I unfolded it into the borax a warning went off,
"You need more adult company."
How do I like motherhood, complete submersion?
My veins are surfacing, auguries on a Delphic map.

You want to crawl into the speakers,
swallow Schubert's Impromptu. Who gave you this hunger
for the world? A stop sign fires your brain
with delight—the octagon and bold letters
burn into you, you want to stay,
run your light fingers over the rusted pole.

Sometimes an awkward adult attempts to amuse you
with peekaboo. You look at him or her to ask
"What did you get your Ph.D. in, irrelevance?
Give me doorknobs to turn, a screen door to push,
a straight look, words to swish in my mouth,
lift me up to see the chandelier, do something practical!"

Crawling eight gallons of milk to the mile,
you want to deform my face, scratch a message
into my chin, my eyes that will last, be your Rushmore.
Nursing you is nursing a windmill,
arms and legs rotary blades,
mouth fixed, the pagan center of the universe, immovable.

You sit without support, fall mouth open,
a piranha onto the nearest part of me,
suck on my shoulder, leave it black and blue.
You crow "abba," Hebrew for father, then "ma,"
not addressing us, but we squeeze as best we can
into the terms you give us. Of course I'd change my name
to be the one you called.

7 Months: Early Nursing

*I have calmed and quieted my soul,
like a child quieted at its mother's breast,
like a child that is quieted is my soul.*
— Psalm 131:2

I woke to find you looking at me, wide-eyed,
as if to see for yourself if you were all here.
Trying with your free hand to detach your right ear,
you nursed eagerly at 4:30 a.m. My husband promptly said
"I'm moving to the guest bed," as if he had programmed himself
to say this without activating the normal speech centers
as he walked, clutching his pillow, out of the bedroom,
congenial, slow moving, resolute, the words "bed"
and "sleep" flashing repeatedly deep in his neural pathways
where the urge to survive is lodged.

I whispered to my daughter, fully awake,
sounds I took for a bowel movement only gas.
When we finished nursing a quiet rain began.
I opened blinds; she crept
to feel cool air come
over arms and token hair, to hear and smell

early rain for the first time.

Her ear's thin curtain curved against the light,
its small slug of wax migrating within my reach.
A mockingbird began, sang her back to sleep.
I watched even light displace the shadows each molecule casts,
the darkened maple, the lightening grass,
and listened for sparrows waking, one by one.

        8 Months: I want to teach you how various clouds

sweep the sky, bring us different weather, how the air
turns with the earth, how the soul turns toward God.

I want to show you different ferns, plumage
of green peacocks, fruitdots releasing spore,

how white cells patrol the blood, how your skin,
a fresh ream of swelling silk, breathes.

Come, see the moon loom through thinning trees,
feel the dark air startle

your lungs, tingle fingers your first fall
outside me. Your planet's shedding clothes for sleep,

bedding down, taking stock.
The season circle will be a waltz for you,

as close as breath, leaves falling
as you rise for the first time to your feet

        9 Months: No one taught us this dance.

I woke five seconds before
you called me in a dream
and am rolling toward you,
semipermeable. Feelings circulate

as if without author, or with two.
I take on your cough, hold you
on my chest, sing you to sleep as you sing
in your own tongue. Who cannot speak?

I do not count on sleeping through a night, or writing or making
love or meditating or taking a shower.
The morning is cold, too cold for your bath,
and you want to be close, to watch your father dress
and go, to lift and tear pages from the mail.
You nurse often, as if regaining memory each time,
as milk and arms flow about you.

You are twenty-nine inches long, almost walking.
I am seventy inches long, almost crawling
to get a closer look in your eyes,
the marbled caves I went into when you were born
to live out of my head
but not insane—
to live somewhere in my heart
where I began.

10 Months: First Fever

You must be held upright to sleep, embraced
through the night, gasping to nurse every three hours,
barking your mucus loose, grabbing my nightgown
you've sweated through to get to my own wet skin.

Pots on the stove steam until the windows cloud;
you cough then cry. I hold you close, waltz
around the living room, tell you we will make it
better, but you know I am crying, though not why:

at the limits of my love, darling, you've shown me
the limits of my love's power.

11 Months: Mute

After eleven months chattering,
giving revues as cereal cooled,
I lost my voice.
Now I can at most whisper
and you do all the talking, pointing, looking at me
for response. "Preehee!" Everything

that catches any light is pretty.
You speak in many tongues, the amalgam
before Babel unwound it. Any language could spin off
your liquid, saliva-spouting, singing talk. You talk more
to make up for my strange silence.
I smile more, dance with you as always, kiss you up
and down your spine. Boat of language,

you are launched, could find any adult now
and draw a tongue out of your all-containing mouth.
Your feelings are twirling into articulate cases;
soon they will be precise, emphatic as tight-fitting gloves.
Words may even coffin some feelings better left
in your first, mother tongue, the one I didn't teach you,

but watched you find. You jammed fingers,
nipples, food, carpet fuzz, book bindings
into that small black triangle, your mouth, to come out
with all the sounds the world needs.
Now I watch them ferrying away. You do not miss
my talking. Soon yours will fill the house
with no help from me. I will be the one reduced
to trying to articulate strange feelings of being left.

12 Months: Living with a Drunk

Falling with dumb grace
you would land perfectly in a parachute,
not knowing enough
or knowing too much to fear. Tumbling down stairs

you stand up unmarked, the soft crown
of your skull pulsing. You want me to hold you

upside down while you tramp on your hands across the room.
Hands high, you dance dervish circles 'til you drop.
Teach me how to fall. You stomp away,
diaper strewn aside. Generalissimo of the carpet,
you point, "Off with that wall!"

    Twenty Months: Weaning

You look me in the eye, scowl,
reluctantly repeat after me,
"The milk has gone away."

I rock you, sing half an hour
until you whisper, "Mama, Mama,"
softer, softer, gone.
Your dreams steam onto the sheet.

I squeeze hurting breasts over the sink:
white tears ooze out.
My calloused nipples, swelling belly
want to attend to the new child inside,
lay down its bones and heart chambers,
not spurt milk for you.

What does the aspen feel
before cells divide to make a fork,
find a second, untried way to the sun?
For the one life I've chosen

seven or eight were begun,
hover invisibly by my shoulder: monastic
teaching, marrying another man, practicing
'cello in a cabin until that Colorado stream
trilled black each night.

Meredith Briggs Skeath

The Hammer's Claw

Prying away sheet rock to inspect for termites,
we found a gap between the wall and floor.
What holds up our house?
The furring strips were filigreed, cinder blocks
out of sight. That night
I found a gap between body and soul.

The body can stop cantering and roll over
like the willful, tired horse who rolled over
on me. I slipped out, watched him
from outside the ring—his large iris darted,
glad to be rid of my weight.
The stable woman insisted I get back on
to "teach him who was boss." I was eleven.
I knew who was boss.

Last night when my daughter woke to nurse at 3 a.m.
I grabbed the railing to get downstairs.
Feeling eighty or older, my body wanted only
to lie down, intention sapped by heavy lungs,
the heart's unending drum roll, vamp music for what?

This morning she twirls hands and feet,
new skin stretching over bone,
follows a patch of sun across the carpet,
chooses a color scheme for the sky
each time she looks up.
Seeing her I think, "I can die now."

Away from her I feel displaced.
She crawls to find me, to say,
"This is heaven enough
for me, isn't it for you?"

You May Not Remember

how my milk tastes, like milk and maple syrup mixed,
nor these hours in embrace, lying together,
your hair, back, legs being stroked,
you twisting my free nipple, poking
the bulging breast, talking to me
while you nursed, emphatic staccato diminishing
into murmur, then sleep. It all sounds sensual,

even sexual. You won't call me your first lover,
or even your first love, but I'll be there
implicitly when you hold your wife, tighter,
pressing yourselves together, pulsing. After all
where did you learn delight? Who showed you touch,
the first alphabet, could spell love?

Meredith Briggs Skeath

Immersion

I fortify the bedroom walls with the maternal:
photos of my grandmother holding me, my mother
holding my daughter, my mother walking me
down the aisle, framed in gold.
This is my office: night,
when no one else hears the rousing child,
the searching mouth. No one faults
or praises me, whatever I do.
These shades spell me, hand me doses
of energy, or patience, like cups of sugar water held out
for the marathoner's shuttling hand.

Nine months waking every two hours for my son; ten.
This has nothing to do with stamina, or a supportive husband,
or conviction. How did my mother
hold our family together? How did my grandmother,
when the depression made violin lessons, even from a virtuoso, expendable,
and my grandfather turned to raising chickens
and melancholia?
   Circling in me,
they make me wake a second before my son,
my daughter, caught in a groundswell of consciousness
   that spreads
across the room, passes over my husband
and lifts me up to carry, change, nurse, console
to sleep. In this world man
is a paltry seeder. The woman makes the soul
at home in its body again and again, night after night.

Yes, my mother answered me, she always answered me,
I never thought
it could be otherwise, her love around me,
an ocean. I drank it, salty.
It became my blood, my life.
That is why I wake whenever I need to—

the maternal calls me and I walk the path cleared
by my mother, my grandmother, all who suckled, swaddled,
laid down every particle of sense and longing
before the secret-laden, illuminated
child. How can I not hear you?
You raise me from living to a joint life,
even our brain waves shared. I hold you,
nurse or simply look you back to sleep.
Come, it is not dawn yet, the stars still want your dreams.

What I Learned Being a Mediocre Bookkeeper

You ask me to settle, close out
accounts. Debits, assets, liabilities—all
in numbers. I juggle, reenter, fuss—
appeal to the wizards of money
to make the numbers that need to
match.

There, we can submit our returns
no one will raise an eyebrow, we look
normal, it will be good
enough.

I am exhausted, balancing scales, tracking
money like droppings across the screen. All this
translates into what I am able to do
for our children, what largess
I can express, what I have left
to be generous with, what opportunities
I can offer.

It is not illusion, this accounting, though dollars
are artifact and the faces on the bills degrade, unknown.
It means options, freedoms, doors opening,
closing. Nothing essential, but something
to respect.

This is why I honor those who dribble
numbers back and forth, because numbers are keys
to doors I wish to open, wide French doors, not to heaven,
(those cost nothing), but to dinners with guests,
lives giving thanks and laughter floating out the windows
up to the stars.

God's Net

FOR JOANNA ARIEL AT NINE

When you leave I throw my love after you
like a net, not to bring you back
from your sleepover
but to surround you,
like the halo the saint.

Darling, willow who asks, "Am I fat?"
doing cartwheels across the living room,
no matter how big you get,
tall, wide, willful, or famous,

this lap will wait,
your first throne; these arms
will open and close for you
like sea fans waving
under warm water.

Others will embrace
and compel you,
but my wrinkled belly, your first home,
my floppy breasts, your first restaurant,
will always fold around you,
simple as a faithful horse.

And when this body goes,
don't worry! You'll be amazed,
relieved, (even laugh out loud!)
to feel, in the midst of grief,
my love, as I did
when my mother "died."
The net remains!

In Hiding

Elizabeth conceived; and she hid herself five months.
— Luke, 1:24

FOR ORALEE ELIZABETH

A father's tremor, your heartbeat,
a thimbleful of blood, waters within the waters
within me. I tell no one.
First build the temple.
The soul will see if it is fit.

Your unknown blood,
darkness within my own,
gushes; I muffle your tiny kicks.
Secret of secrets! I ask you not to enter your body

until the doctor has needled your waters,
found all undamaged. Then enter triumphant
as David, dancing on the streets of Jerusalem,
for God.

Penumbra, felt about me, we will not hurry.
Cartilage is being replaced by bone,
toes are billowing out of stubs.
Your body is old enough to urinate.
I clean your waters
continually. Who can part us,
watching the fittings, the lintel, the curves
of the brain blooming?

I bulge. My daughter starts a quilt for you.
I touch the new leaves, new moss, fiddleheads,
hungry for your skin.

Spring rains glut the stream, grass spurts out of mud,
worms swim onto sidewalks. The waters, the waters
have magnified me. I shall gather my silences round
my silvering head, lay baskets of joy before the Lord!

III. Courted by God

And underneath <u>are</u> the everlasting arms.
— Deuteronomy 33:27

Meredith Briggs Skeath

Unexpected Call

    As if my love were calling
Come, come to me,
then moving off through olive trees,
I could not see him or hear
his words, only sense the tone
of his longing, how it eddied
the air.

    I felt, not words,
but the melted, single yearning one love has
for another. How could God
long for me? I thought all the courting
would be mine to do.

Lovers seek the farthest outcropping
where surf comes, close and cold
with wind-spray mingling their hair
when they bend close, as they must,
to hear each other's words that near
the working sea.
When I close my eyes I think
this is between God and me, for now
the world can fall away.

Before and After Eating

I never wanted to be caught off guard: I was willing
to look at anything head on--such as a lobster
midway into the pot, its beaded eyes projecting
from the chef's hairy hand that held it as main entreé
of an $18.95 dinner, not the creature used
to dark bottom. Looking in one eye, I wanted to buy
the last two slow moving ones at the bottom of the tank
and take them out to Chesapeake Bay,
just as I wanted to take along the nodding man
on the sidewalk downtown, the one we passed at 11 p.m.
on the way home from our inspiring meeting.
He was leaning on his knees on a store stoop,
behind a shopping cart full of plastic bags.
A wind break? A hedge? A plea of metal
and plastic, the bars a scale without notes.

I asked you if you ever had the impulse
to take a street person home. You paused, said no.
We were driving through the prostitute section
of 14th street. Hurrying, you turned down a one-way
the wrong way. A few blocks later, behind a bus,
fumes turned me nauseous. When we got home
our tank was leaking, only the moon and one star
showed through the haze. Our street was uneventful,
oak lined. After you lay down
to sleep, I sat up, tears coming without reason,
feeling without words, for the dying I have taken
into myself and uselessly become.

Meredith Briggs Skeath

Outside the Orchard

At dinner I asked for a newspaper.
(A poem of mine, someone had said,
might be printed there.) It was,
inexplicably, on page one,
not buried beside the changes
in school lunch menus. Nothing
but the poem was on the front page—
of a paper already handed out
to a thousand people I didn't know.

I walked out into the evening, glad
the people I passed were strangers.
I didn't want to be with anyone like myself,
but alone with someone great,
someone I might understand through study
and silence, such as Emily Dickinson,
were it possible to approach her
renaming the world by herself
in her Amherst orchard.

I walked to a drift of pines at a nearby lake,
apart from people and light,
to feel the wind I have always listened to
move across the landscape
heading for open fields and space.

Only a few words I've heard or read
command attention not from dread but love,
as if they deserved to be carried by the wind.
Like an owl's primary feathers sculpting the air
they make the wind serve their purpose.
But most words, surely most of mine,
don't travel far.

Soultending

When I read my poems to an audience
their applause touched me, momentarily stirred
the air. But I thought of Emily
in her orchard at dusk, not to pick
the Jonathans or Winesaps, but to smell
and feel their skins at that hour.
With a hint of a sidelong glance from her
within my mind, I left the hall and went outside
to the night air, to my life again.

Meredith Briggs Skeath

Hunting Abstractions

"What distinguishes human beings," the likable
sociology professor began, "is the ability to abstract.
When I say tree, for instance, does anyone think
of a particular tree? No."

I was lost. I thought of a particular tree, the Dutch elm
I grew up with. Before umbrella or vase showed me that shape,
it lifted up, out and down; before fountains,
before French horns, the elm stood wired together,
holding on, bending over the roof, the street,
a gesture of blessing caught in form.

I felt its welted bark where our sleds and dog gnawed it.
I watched its particular branches sleep, flinging seeds,
leaves, sights of the night sky.
It arrested me, even in thought,
and beauty was whatever enabled it to stop
my abstract blur, pierce my labelling of time and type,
until I stood in my mind alone, unlike any anatomy
illustration I'd seen, rooted as the elm in soil
of my own peculiar making, able to see each tree
without precedent, without a duplicate
waiting to be called into service, reliable
(and boring) as an emergency gas tank.

My professor later went to the breeding grounds
of the Adelaide penguins to find out how each penguin
identified its mate and offspring among 40,000+
inhabitants of what he called the "city of nuns."
Undoubtedly his down parka ballooned
in the antarctic wind and he was stopped short,
at least at first, by complete barrenness, by his breath
icing his binoculars, and the subtle differences
he had come to find but could not detect
in a sea of wings and bodies, cries and gestures.

In his absence I passed three hunters who did not think
of particular geese, as he predicted,
though each goose mates for life
and does not mate again if its mate dies. I shouted
when geese flew over my house, if the hunters were near.
I used garbage can lids as cymbals to drive the birds
back to their swamp. When shots rang out I prayed
they missed, but one goose fell from formation,
suddenly 30 pounds of flesh, no wings.
Its mate wavered, started to follow it down,
then flew back up amidst a second volley.
The goose fell loudly to the waiting setters.
The weekend hunters were understandably proud
of their marksmanship, their cunning
in luring the geese with mock cries,
but to me they had stolen something that belonged
to the sky, that made it speak, specifically, of heaven.

Meredith Briggs Skeath

Sleeping Under Dogs

On freezing nights the arthritic setter recovering
from a stroke and the frenetic young pointer are hauled
into the kitchen over our heads. We turn out our light
under paws clinking across linoleum.
The sound of two or three wooden folding chairs
collapsing is the old setter lying down.

They wake at random hours, lick themselves, slap the floor
with their tails, and only they hear
our lovemaking, another way of breathing, another alphabet
they know is human below them.
When the man two floors up comes down at dawn
they yap, convulse, collide
into cabinets to be let out, bolt

to our door to jump on us. With no idea
they've been our ceiling and gate
clanking us open from sleep, they've kept the animal
awake in us–gentle, wild, or simply rocking

on our haunches. Shedding tufts, fur
the colors of burning leaves and ash, they careen
around the yard, look for escape, snatch
rawhide strips I slip them at odd moments,
like this, rewarding them in cold sun
not for manners or for being quiet
or intelligent–just for being.

Attempted Translation

I was up before anyone, reading alone, the dawn
    gathering humidity
as if it were the momentum necessary to make a day.
The breeze, not yet hot, parcelled itself through the screen,
when I noticed the Japanese maple outside the window
    waving slowly,
moving as if in another world, to a different music
    than I could hear.
It was saying something, not consciously to me,
    but something,
and I was the mute, the one without equivalent words, the one
who couldn't hear the message clearly, only know
    it was there.

How often trees, birds spoke to me as a child—
Florida jays came to prick my palm with their claws
    and feed, chickadees
    answered my mimicking whistle.
I was sure theirs was a language as rich, perhaps
    richer than mine,
if I could only learn it. The world was sentient.
    The clouds were not omens,
not messages sent expressly for me by some god,
but something better—silent yet complete disclosures
    of themselves,
holding back nothing.

The maple's leaves had emerged like folded hands,
    their fingers pointed down
and notched, and I had watched them open, like butterflies
climbing wet from the chrysalises. This slight tree,
planted too close to the house, under the shadow
    of an imposing pine
in a cramped city yard, had nothing to say
of what was beyond itself. It lived in the flow of fluids

up its capillaries, opening and closing its lips
on the underside of each leaf, the immense
breathing in and out, putting oxygen on our table,
that we might live, sending it into the windows, taking
    our exhaust
back into itself. Its root hairs edged against the foundation,
parting the earth like slow, microscopic worms,
    anchoring a life.

A woman who loved flowers had planted it
    about forty years ago,
a woman who had not learned how to space trees,
and she put it close to the house and the pine
    so she could see them both
against the window. But the tree did not speak of the past,
I only guessed it had been planted on purpose, the only one
    of its kind
on the block. Its leaves shifted in air like thoughts against
    a backdrop,
like feelings shifting in silence, it moved like a slow dancer
brushing the screen, and spoke of quietness by being it.

Wastebasket

Ringlets of reed twined by some noticably human hand
that made (God be thanked) mistakes
so that holes of different sizes appear
in its side—this is the basket I paid for,
knowing I would never need another.

Round and deep, sturdy enough
for all the trash I heave and sail
into its mouth: ships, gliders, casually falling showers
of scrap confetti, drafts all settle, like snow on layer
of snow in the Andes where the basket came from.

I wanted to pay the woman or man who made it,
not the clerk in the store, but the hardening hands,
automatic, that bent it—thank them
for the rim and holes that let me see through
all I want to lose, the vacant well
that leaves me free from my mistakes, a new dance
on bare feet each morning.

Cleanser of my mind, like sleep or meditation,
I give you all the drippings of my desk, the clippings
yellowing from the times, the letters from old intimates,
the pictures of godchildren who've grown up,
and you receive it, hold it armlessly, quietly,
lull it to sleep before the burning.

Meredith Briggs Skeath

What My Coach Said Before the Reading

Don't slur the words as if they were polysyllabic ingredients
of a cake mix or toxins from the chart
of chemical elements. Give each its due,
enough force and space so it can sink
with its load into silence.

And remember what your father said after hearing
your first lecture: "Meredith, it was fine,
but you have the gestures of an Italian cab driver."
I had to tie your arms with flesh-colored stockings
to the podium, until they were trained as braces train teeth.
Please don't revive your papal arm spreading now.

Instead, pick out a person in each corner of the room
and speak to him, not just to the cheering
first line I've planted.

Who are you talking to? By the end, if you're good,
you'll know. Take responsibility for the words
that fail. Put the good ones under the credits
of the one in you who was writing
before you were born. Now go,
send your words straight, like a transfusion, to the heart.

Vitae

> *The trap door fell open and I fell through, out of my life's story, both its blessing and burden.*

Where do I live?
Not in a house, not in time.

What is my name?
Not what I thought, not the ones given,
not the ones taken.

What is my face?
Not emotions' map, the wrinkles
I've earned.

What compels me?
Love given, love called
for me to give.

Will you find me?
When you are
utterly still—

but completely alive—
Yes. You will find me.

Meredith Briggs Skeath

August Morning

Early morning air, the least polluted,
is saturated. Cricket voices recede
like nuns going out after a service.
Crows and cars take over.

I go out to brush my hair by the tomato plant
climbing into the lilac bush, to feel the air,
the presence of God walking in the garden.

I invite Him into my heart,
beating like the sea. He is already there.
I invite Him into my house, in need of repair

but filled with sincere yearning.
He is already there.
I invite Him to watch over all in trouble.
It is already done.

Papers thud on each set of front steps
like heavily footed soldiers marching,
all carrying the same stories
of an ordinary August morning.

Owning Up

Faith—as good as a ground walnut shell
to a starving squirrel. I speak only
from experience.

If the telescope sees far
I will tell you what I see.
I won't make up the color of the beaches

or the dress of the natives
in the next world.
I'll tell you where my knowledge,

that spit of knowing, ends.
But I will also tell you the source of my blessings,
the Lord who delivers challah to my house,

throws a shawl of love
over my shaking shoulders.
I will not disown Him by refusing to name

His finger upon my chest, in my viscera, my checkbook,
my garden--rendering nothing mine, all His.
If you can hear I will speak

for what dog can resist wagging her tail
mightily when her good master bends down
and cradles her jowls in his hand?